Remember Lot's Wife

Give up the world and don't look back!

BY
CHARLES PRETLOW

Remember Lot's Wife
Give up the world and don't look back!

First printing November 2010
Copyright © Charles Pretlow

All rights reserved. Printed in the United States of America. No part of this publication may be reproduced, stored in a retrieval system, or transmitted, in any form or by any means electronic, mechanical, photocopying, recording, or otherwise, without the prior written permission of the author.

All scripture references and quotes are from the Revised Standard Version of the Holy Bible unless otherwise noted.
Old Testament Section Copyright © 1952
New Testament Section Copyright © 1946, 1971
by Thomas Nelson Inc.

ISBN 978-0-9801768-5-8

Published by -
Wilderness Voice Publishing
Colorado USA
www.wildernesspublishing.com

About WVP Tract-Book Series

Wilderness Voice Publishing brings this series of short messages on sound doctrine and Christ's teachings to help the sincere Christian shed the many last day false teachings and become mature in the true Christ.

These books are designed to meet the needs of individual disciples, workers, and ministries helping each to become ready for a true and final move of God before Christ appears.

Each book focuses on a specific issue that troubles and confuses many believers today and causes harm to their relationship with Christ. Each author has worked out these very issues qualifying them to bring forth a sound teaching, rightly handling the word of truth. Wilderness Voice Publishing only publishes authors who refuse to tamper with Scripture, taking passages out of context and twisting their true meaning.

We encourage the reader to carefully study all scripture references and seek the Lord for a clear understanding with a willingness to embrace His discipline.

"For the word (written) of God is living and active, sharper than any two-edged sword, piercing to the division of soul and spirit, of joints and marrow, and discerning the thoughts and intentions of the heart. And before him no creature is hidden, but all are open and laid bare to the eyes of him with whom we have to do" (Hebrews 4:12, 13).

To that end, may we all *"attain to the unity of the faith and of the knowledge of God, to mature manhood, to the measure of the stature of the fullness of Christ; so that we may no longer be children, tossed to and fro and carried about by every wind of doctrine, by the cunning of men, by their craftiness in deceitful wiles"* (Ephesians 4:13, 14).

Contents

Jesus Said, *"Remember Lot's Wife"* **7**
Why did Lot's Wife Look Back? **8**
Trouble will Wake Up Spellbound Christians. **13**
Final Awaking and Coming Away. **15**
Give Up the World and Don't Look Back. **18**
Enduring To the End. **20**
Are You Destined for God's Wrath? **25**

About the Author. **29**
Ministry Information. **30**
More Books by the Author. **31**
Other Tract-Book Titles. **33**

JESUS SAID, "REMEMBER LOT'S WIFE"

"Likewise as it was in the days of Lot—they ate, they drank, they bought, they sold, they planted, they built, but on the day when Lot went out from Sodom fire and sulphur rained from heaven and destroyed them all—so will it be on the day when the Son of man is revealed. On that day, let him who is on the housetop, with his goods in the house, not come down to take them away; and likewise let him who is in the field not turn back. Remember Lot's wife. Whoever seeks to gain his life will lose it, but whoever loses his life will preserve it. I tell you, in that night there will be two in one bed; one will be taken and the other left. There will be two women grinding together; one will be taken and the other left. Two men will be in the field, one will be taken and the other left" (Luke 17:28-36).

Christ saw the last days as terrible, yet normal. He saw Christians taking their ease, living happily in the world with God's blessings. Our Lord warned to beware of this condition of heart throughout His prophecies and parables concerning the last day Christian. Even though trouble increases—most of the world will live a normal life, building, marrying, selling, planting and carrying on *as usual!*

The free world's prosperity and temporal blessings, especially in America, Canada, the United Kingdom, and Europe, has a death grip upon the spirits and souls of most Christians! Jesus foresaw this and warned!

Good-hearted Christians are clinging to this world, many putting their eternal salvation at risk or at least storing up for themselves and their family unnecessary trouble. Their hearts are weighed down with the cares of this life and risk missing the rapture. Few read and take to heart these particular warnings of Christ. Many gloss over these warnings because they have been told not to worry about the end of the age—Christ has everything under control and you'll be raptured to safety before trouble comes your way.

The goodness of the world has a spellbinding power upon the normal Christian who desires to serve Christ and get along in this world. Many a Christian's heart is not prepared for Christ's return, and all the trouble leading up to His appearing.

Far too many Christians love the goodness of the world more than they love God. That is why Christ warned concerning *Lot's wife*.

Lot's wife was told in no uncertain terms—"Don't look back!" So, why is Christ using Lot's wife as a warning for the last day Christian, to not look back? The answer is in why Lot's wife looked back.

Why did Lot's Wife Look Back?

What made Lot's wife look back? Lot's wife did not look back at Sodom because of its evil or because she missed evil. She looked back because of her sentimentality toward the good that she had experienced as she and her family lived amongst that generation of evil people in Sodom.

All of us have been blessed by others who are nice and do *good*, or appear to be good in the world, but many of these so-called good people have no interest in God or the things of God. These are the *good-*

looking evil people in the world who tolerate and even condone evil in others, though they themselves might not practice evil. An evil generation will proclaim God and look very good on the outside, serving God in talk, not in deed. There is a difference between the truly righteous and those who appear to be righteous.

We see many *good people* protest against certain evils such as war, abortion, and other disturbing or bad things such as capital punishment.

Most that are squeamish have chosen a "live and let live" philosophy for life, learning to tolerate and give concession to evil. King Saul had this attitude of heart, leading him to disobey God's orders. We see this same concession enveloping many nations, families and far too often many within congregations everywhere.

Many pastors and ministers are afraid to call evil, evil and chase out the wolves. So concessions are made, evil is tolerated and often ignored. Peter confronted Ananias and Sapphira concerning their satanic evil devices and as a result they died instantly. Ask yourself this, how many in Christian leadership would confront evil as Peter did? How many *good* people would protest the death of Ananias and Sapphira?

So here is the issue with Lot's wife, she had made concessions within her heart concerning the *good* people of Sodom. She had fond memories of her relationships with the *good-looking evil people* in Sodom. This same condition holds true with many Christians today who also have fond memories and nice feelings from worldly relationships, living, working, playing; all these activities helping to form friendship with those of the world.

James warded, *"Do you not know that friendship with the world is enmity with God? Therefore whoever wishes to be a friend of the world makes himself an enemy of God"* (James 4:4).

All these things have a spellbinding power upon the heart of a Christian as the end of the age draws near. Lot's wife was warned and she began her journey to safety only to disobey and become frozen in her tracks, turning to salt. Most likely, in her heart she could not believe God would destroy *the good* with the *bad*. You see, self-righteous people who practice good can be as wicked as those we consider bad that practice evil.

Remember the parable that Christ told concerning the tax collector and the righteous man on the way to the temple? (See Luke 18:9-14).

Why does God want separation from the world and death to the love of the world?

Simply—the world is fashioned after Satan's nature—lust of the eye, pride of life, lust of the flesh, tolerance of sin and evil, manipulation, competition, jealousy, selfish ambition, control and deceit.

This is the condition many Christians are stuck in as the end of the age unfolds. When Christ calls, many will be unable to go—as their hearts resist separating and departing from *the good* in a lost, dying and rebellious world. How many are ready in their innermost heart to let go now. How many Christians will be ready when the time comes?

Jesus tells us not to be alarmed at what takes place leading up to the beginning of the events that start the end-of-the-age. We are now in wars and rumors of wars as well as natural upheavals, Jesus called these birth pangs and not to be alarmed, but He does warn of the coming persecution, a great falling away, where putting Christians to death will be widespread and the growth of terrible wickedness.

Christ is warning Christians that at a certain time a massive persecution will come as the world turns against true Christians. Persecution will grow throughout the nations of the world and anti-Christian sentiment will increase within world governments.

False and liberal Christians will hate the true Christian who cries out, warns and defies the coming New World Order. Of course, Muslims, and other world religions will become even more hateful toward Christians. The current Iraqi and Afghani wars are galvanizing deep hatred throughout the world toward Jews and Christians. The Muslim world perceives that America and Israel are Christian and Jewish countries conspiring to rule their world.

The world as a whole is moving increasingly toward socialism where individual rights and freedoms are relinquished to government dominance, both in the private lives of their citizens and in business. Free enterprise and free trade will begin to disappear. Government will control more and more of our everyday life. All this is leading to the New World Order and the rise of the antichrist.

There is an awful time coming for Christians! Most will not stand during this time, unless they get ready.

God's people are held spellbound by the "goodness" and "prosperity" we so cherish. It is hard for the sincere Christian to grasp the fact that evil is very pervasive and insidious, ready to be released in every level of society and across all nations. Much *good* is used to cover-up an evil heart. We find it hard to believe that God expects Christians to separate themselves from such—before judgment falls. In fact, many find it incomprehensible that God will judge the so-called *good* in the world. Jesus said, *"He who is not with me is against me, and he who does not gather with me scatters"* (Matthew 12:30).

As I share the many accounts concerning our confrontations with evil most Christians are surprised, perplexed and frankly doubt the validity of our battles. Remember, evil often comes in a cloak of decency!

We have found it necessary to completely let go of our false perception of the world as being *good* in order to recognize and fight hidden evil. Yes, we are to look for the good, but not to be deceived by the false good and the deception of the world. *"Look carefully then how you walk, not as unwise men but as wise, making the most of the time, because the days are evil"* (Ephesians 5:15,16).

God will break the spell over His people concerning the goodness of the world. God is trying to awaken the foolish and unprepared Christian to these issues and forebodings of trouble. Countless exposés of vile evil have surfaced throughout society and throughout Christian churches. These things will continue along with increased societal immorality.

These birth pangs, the coming persecution, and the Great Tribulation are God's way of awakening His people to get ready. He will shake everything that can be shaken. (See Hebrews 12:26-29).

Not too many Christians agree that Catholicism is the worst of all cults. Even as this corrupt false church is being exposed, this cult is still sanctioned throughout evangelical, charismatic and even many

Pentecostal denominations and individual fellowships as a valid Christian denomination. This is the result of Satan's plan. The end of the age harlot church, consisting of unified Protestant denominations and Catholics, drawing millions of wayward and unsuspecting Christians into the devil's grip.

The world says, "All roads to God are valid" and those who say otherwise are now suspect and will soon be considered opponents of the coming New World Order. Many Christians will be in the valley of decision long before the mark of the beast comes. Regrettably, many will choose a *New World false Christian and religious order* that fosters unity at the expense of embracing and teaching the true gospel of Christ.

Even now, the so-called Emerging Church led by a handful of Mega-Church pastors, inspired by the likes of Rick Warren of Saddle Back Church, Brian McLaren and others are leading many down this apostate path.

Trouble will Wake Up Spellbound Christians

More personal trouble, persecution, a Sodomite society and demonic oppression will awaken those who have faith but are spellbound. The false Christians who have shipwrecked their faith will take the full plunge and sell their birthrights to get along with a persecuting, hate-filled world.

Right now the mission of many misguided Christians is sanitizing the world. If the world is somewhat moral, then it is easy to justify having an inordinate love of the world, with its deceitful trappings of goodness. This is rooted in the pursuit of worldly success, pleasure and prosperity. Indeed, this is an aspect of caring for the world in a way that weighs down the heart.

The prosperity message is in conflict with God's Spirit and soon this contradiction will either sear the conscience completely or free the Christian. Christians who wake up in time will stop trying to purify Disneyland and the *magic kingdom*, and prepare themselves and *get ready* for the coming kingdom of God.

We are to be salt of the earth—not purifiers of the world, trying to make the world a sinless, sanitized place where the whole world is converted to Christianity. This ideology comes from embracing false doctrine that contradicts Christ's warnings concerning the end of the age.

"But the day of the Lord will come like a thief, and then the heavens will pass away with a loud noise, and the elements will be dissolved with fire, and the earth and the works that are upon it will be burned up. Since all these things are thus to be dissolved, what sort of persons ought you to be in lives of holiness and godliness, waiting for and hastening the coming of the day of God, because of which the heavens will be kindled and dissolved, and the elements will melt with fire!" (2 Peter 3:10-12).

Great persecution for Christians in the so-called "free world" is about to be unleashed. What many of our brethren have experienced in the communist countries and third-world Islamic nations will soon come to us! Believe me—this is right around the corner.

This trend is already beginning and will certainly adjust the lukewarm Christian's priorities and

Give up the world and don't look back!

attitude. A sifting is coming through persecution that will separate the weeds (or tares) from the wheat.

Persecution, along with other catastrophic problems that are coming, will break the budget of thousands of churches and fellowships across North America. Phony TV ministries will run short of money as the true body of Christ shapes up and pays attention to the leaner true ministries that are providing sound doctrine and honest leadership.

Final Awaking and Coming Away

Home churches will start springing up everywhere. Hunger to meet with like-minded Christians will destroy the desire to be entertained with false worship and ear-tickling messages that miss the mark. True Christians will become nauseated with the lukewarm hypocrite as they spew out poison every time they open their mouth. A desire to discern and separate oneself from the phony and the world has already begun and will continue to grow, leading to a pure and powerful church—the bride of Christ.

Yes, true discipleship training and teachings will be the priority of those coming out from the false system of worship across America—called "Churchianity."

A Christian exodus is about to begin as millions of Christians turn from the false to the true—and conversely, millions of phony Christians will seek out the harlot false denominations that still hold the form of godliness but deny the true power of God.

Many places of worship will wake up, set priorities straight and begin to make disciples of Christ rather than followers of denominations, leaders and exotic movements. Many will realize that these man-made sectarian doctrines, flamboyant leaders, and exotic movements did nothing to help prepare them for the trouble they will be forced to endure.

Yes, trouble is coming and we must be prepared to endure to the end and be saved: to be saved from unnecessary trouble, to be saved from being left behind, to be saved from an unclean heart that would look back when the final trumpet is blown.

Like Lot's wife, many are looking back. Lot's wife left with her husband and family, but her heart clung to Sodom. Again, it was the *good* things to which her *heartstrings* were tied. Like Lot's wife, many Christians have their hearts connected to this world for a variety of reasons, which may all seem legitimate. These Christians, perhaps even some of you who are reading this message, are unconsciously connected to this world.

Christ's simple statement, *"Remember Lot's wife,"* is a clear message for Christians who have the same condition of heart that caused this woman to look back. Like Lot's wife, these Christians are coming out and being identified with Christ and His teachings. They seem stable, walking away from sin and unhealthy relationships, nevertheless these Christians whom Christ warns of are in danger of being left behind.

Are you looking back in your heart of hearts? Perhaps you are spellbound with carnal relationships and how life used to be. Sentimentality is one of Satan's strongholds, concerning Christ's warning not to look back. We all have fond memories of the good times, pleasant memories of childhood, filled with picnics, outings and so on.

Give up the world and don't look back!

Many reminisce with deep sentiment over how it used to be growing up. Nostalgia of the good times is ever growing as more and more stress, vile entertainment and supposed pleasurable events become shallow and unfulfilling. Many others have sentimental sorrow over past mistakes such as divorce, a lost childhood due to abuse, missed opportunities and mistakes. Give it all up! Look to the coming age and Christ's soon return. *Get ready*!

Don't pretend these issues are not there, but resolve the pain, sentiment, and cares of the heart. You may need to weep and mourn over these unresolved wounds, emotional ties and lusts. Pretending away or shrink-wrapping these issues will cause you to be caught off-guard. These things are what Lot's wife was consumed with and caused her to look back.

You may be looking forward to Christ's soon return but are looking back in sentimentality and nostalgia, clinging to the good things in the world and to the way it used to be, or the way you would like it to be. This is a doomed world and we must walk as foreigners who long for heaven and Christ's return. We must enjoy in appropriate portion God's blessings but simultaneously and continually break from the bonds of this world's lie.

Lot's wife was not sinning or wanting to live in sin. That is how many Christians live, avoiding sin but loving the world. But, just as Lot's wife had a weight within her heart that caused her demise, so too, many Christians are weighted down.

How many Christians will look up, begin to rise with the last trumpet sound and maybe go a few hundred feet through the air in the rapture, then look back, fall to earth and be left behind—dead!

Let us set aside every weight that so easily besets us and press on in the discipline of the Lord and not wallow in our sentiment and unhealthy worldly affections. Hebrews chapter 12 gives great insight concerning worldly affections and the discipline of the lord.

Give Up the World and Don't Look Back

Lot's wife could not give up friendship with those in Sodom. Many Christians have become friends to this world.

John warns believers concerning loving the world more than God by stating *"Do not love the world or the things in the world. If anyone loves the world, love for the Father is not in him. For all that is in the world, the lust of the flesh and the lust of the eyes and the pride of life, is not of the Father but is of the world. And the world passes away, and the lust of it; but he who does the will of God abides for ever* (1 John 2:15-17).

To be able to stand in these coming days, the true disciple must deal with the things of the world that remain in the heart. Every sincere Christian must dissolve his or her love and friendship with this world.

Christians were told that they need to be "born again," and rightly so, but that rebirth must be of God and one must then grow up into salvation. Many felt a spiritual experience; however their hunger for God and obtaining His righteousness ended there.

They never grew up into salvation, having dealt with the world, the flesh and the pride of life. They think they have a "ticket to ride" when the rapture

Give up the world and don't look back! 19

occurs, but they cannot be further from the truth. These words from the apostle John hold true for the last hour Christians:

How many Christians think they are following Christ and doing God's will, yet are letting the cares of life direct them? Many follow Christ for the blessings and never give up the world.

"As they were going along the road, a man said to him, 'I will follow you wherever you go.' And Jesus said to him, 'Foxes have holes, and birds of the air have nests; but the Son of man has nowhere to lay his head.' To another he said, 'Follow me.' But he said, 'Lord, let me first go and bury my father.' But he said to him, 'Leave the dead to bury their own dead; but as for you, go and proclaim the kingdom of God.' Another said, 'I will follow you, Lord; but let me first say farewell to those at my home.' Jesus said to him, 'No one who puts his hand to the plow and looks back is fit for the kingdom of God'" (Luke 9:57-62).

If you're worried about your retirement, stocks, homes, cars and your family, you must deal with these things in your heart now! They will crowd out Christ and you will find yourself unprepared spiritually to navigate in the coming tribulation. Deal with it now and do not look back, for Jesus said, *"As it was in the days of Noah, so will it be in the days of the Son of man. They ate, they drank, they married, they were given in marriage, until the day when Noah entered the ark, and the flood came and destroyed them all. Likewise as it was in the days of Lot—they ate, they drank, they bought, they sold, they planted, they built, but on the day when Lot went out from Sodom fire and sulphur rained from heaven and destroyed them all—so will it be on the day when the Son of* man is revealed. On that day, let him who is on the housetop, with his goods in the house, not come down to take them away; and likewise let him who is in the field not turn back. Remember Lot's wife"* (Luke 17:26-32).

Another Scripture underscoring this truth reads, *"And he told them a parable: 'Look at the fig tree, and all the trees; as soon as they come out in leaf, you see for yourselves and know that the summer is already near. So also, when you see these things taking place, you know that the kingdom of God is near. Truly, I say to you, this generation will not pass away till all has taken place. Heaven and earth will pass away, but my words will not pass away. But take heed to yourselves <u>lest your hearts be weighed down with dissipation and drunkenness and cares of this life, and that day come upon you suddenly like a snare</u>; for it will come upon all who dwell upon the face of the whole earth. But watch at all times, praying that you [may have strength] to escape all these things that will take place, and to stand before the Son of man'"* (Luke 21:29-36 underline added).

Enduring To the End

"And to the angel of the church in Philadelphia write: 'The words of the holy one, the true one, who has the key of David, who opens and no one shall shut, who shuts and no one opens. I know your works. Behold, I have set before you an open door, which no one is able to shut; I know that you have but little power, and yet you have kept my word and have not denied my name. Behold, I will make those of the synagogue of Satan who say that they are

Jews and are not, but lie—behold, I will make them come and bow down before your feet, and learn that I have loved you. <u>Because you have kept my word of patient endurance, I will keep you from the hour of trial, which is coming on the whole world, to try those who dwell upon the earth</u>. I am coming soon; hold fast what you have, so that no one may seize your crown. He who conquers, I will make him a pillar in the temple of my God; never shall he go out of it, and I will write on him the name of my God, and the name of the city of my God, the new Jerusalem which comes down from my God out of heaven, and my own new name. He who has an ear, let him hear what the Spirit says to the churches"' (Revelation 3:7-13 underline added).

Again, in the coming days the true Christian will be challenged on all sides. Every believer who commits to an all out relationship with Jesus will come under spiritual oppression, various afflictions, and persecution. In fact, at moments, the intensity will be so great it will seem God himself has come against us.

We struggle in our trials because suffering and discipline is foreign to us, but as we endure each trial we can see how meaningful and sovereign the discipline of the Lord truly is.

It will be hard to deny the temptation to quit or compromise. Many will find friends and family members become spiteful, callous, and even treacherous. At times the pressure in relationships, finances, ministry, and trying circumstances will seem unbearable.

In Acts it describes part of Barnabas and Paul's ministry as, *"strengthening the souls of the disciples, exhorting them to continue in the faith, and saying that through many tribulations we must enter the kingdom of God"* (Acts 14:22).

Christian, we are at war. Scripture states that Satan has come down to make war upon the saints; and we must accept reality that in this war, to be a soldier of Christ, there is suffering. *"Share in suffering as a good soldier of Christ Jesus. No soldier on service gets entangled in civilian pursuits, since his aim is to satisfy the one who enlisted him"* (2 Timothy 2:3,4).

Suffering is part of fighting and learning to endure with patience. This is how we develop Christ-like character. It is this character that helps us overcome. *"More than that, we rejoice in our sufferings, knowing that suffering produces endurance, and endurance produces character, and character produces hope, and hope does not disappoint us, because God's love has been poured into our hearts through the Holy Spirit which has been given to us"* (Romans 5:3-6).

When we learn to patiently endure suffering we become steadfast in all of life. *"Count it all joy, my brethren, when you meet various trials, for you know that the testing of your faith produces steadfastness. And let steadfastness have its full effect, that you may be perfect and complete, lacking in nothing"* (James 1:2-4).

Even as we work out our salvation, dealing with our carnal issues, we are admonished to keep our confidence to the end that we might receive what is promised. *"For we share in Christ, if only we hold our first confidence firm to the end"* (Hebrews 3:14).

In our suffering and discipline, God is treating us as a true son or daughter, *"For the Lord disciplines him whom he loves, and chastises every son whom he receives. It is for discipline that you have to endure. God is treating you as sons; for what son is there whom his father does not discipline? If you are left without discipline, in which all have participated, then you are illegitimate children and not sons"* (Hebrews 12:7, 8).

Do not be discouraged when you witness other Christians prospering in false doctrine and indulging in the pleasures of life. They are told to take their ease and be blessed with material wealth and prosperity. The terrible truth is; if they do not awaken in time, His day will come upon them like a snare. *"But take heed to yourselves lest your hearts be weighed down with dissipation and drunkenness and cares of this life, and that day come upon you suddenly like a snare; for it will come upon all who dwell upon the face of the whole earth. But watch at all times, praying that you [may have strength] to escape all these things that will take place, and to stand before the Son of man."* (Luke 21:34-36).

So, as you and I struggle in learning to endure suffering and embrace His discipline, we will receive strength to escape that coming day.

"Therefore we ourselves boast of you in the churches of God for your steadfastness and faith in all your persecutions and in the afflictions which you are enduring. This is evidence of the righteous judgment of God, that you may be made worthy of the kingdom of God, for which you are suffering— since indeed God deems it just to repay with affliction those who afflict you, and to grant rest with us to you

who are afflicted, when the Lord Jesus is revealed from heaven with his mighty angels in flaming fire inflicting vengeance upon those who do not know God and upon those who do not obey the gospel of our Lord Jesus. They shall suffer the punishment of eternal destruction and exclusion from the presence of the Lord and from the glory of his might, when he comes on that day to be glorified in his saints, and to be marveled at in all who have believed, because our testimony to you was believed. To this end we always pray for you, that our God may make you worthy of his call, and may fulfill every good resolve and work of faith by his power, so that the name of our Lord Jesus may be glorified in you, and you in him, according to the grace of our God and the Lord Jesus Christ" (2 Thessalonians 1:4-12).

Indeed, we suffer for the kingdom of God, being made worthy of His call, and to walk in true faith by His power!

Satan will use our own unresolved issues, especially self-pity and hidden unbelief. Thoughts like, *"this is too hard... it's not fair, this is too much... God has forsaken me,"* are tip of the iceberg indicators. Do not ignore these thoughts, but press to the root of each as they come to your awareness.

Evil people cloaked in decency and unrepentant lukewarm Christians become strong weapons used by the enemy. Avoid involvement with such. They will attack your faith, drain you of the *zōē* life in Christ and distract you from doing God's perfect will.

Have consistent fellowship with like-minded Christians. Hold each other accountable and watch each other's back. Always be alert.

Christ is the pioneer and perfecter of our faith, He will not fail us. *"And I am sure that he who began a good work in you will bring it to completion at the day of Jesus Christ"* (Philippians 1:6).

"Who shall separate us from the love of Christ? Shall tribulation, or distress, or persecution, or famine, or nakedness, or peril, or sword? As it is written, 'For thy sake we are being killed all the day long; we are regarded as sheep to be slaughtered.' No, in all these things we are more than conquerors through him who loved us. For I am sure that neither death, nor life, nor angels, nor principalities, nor things present, nor things to come, nor powers, nor height, nor depth, nor anything else in all creation, will be able to separate us from the love of God in Christ Jesus our Lord" (Romans 8:35-39).

Are You Destined for God's Wrath?

This message may seem difficult to bear for some of you. I will not apologize. The sound teachings of Christ and the rest of the word of God support everything I have written here. If it has distressed you, then praise God! There may be time enough for you to get ready; however, there is not that much time left. Playing church is not going to prepare you for the coming hard times.

This is a warning to all of us who are hearing the footsteps of Christ's soon return. Let us not be foolish and be barred from entering into the great celebration on the day that He appears.

The Great Tribulation will force many Christians to buy into Satan's scheme. If we are prepared in our hearts to hear from God rightly and have become true disciples, then we will be able to endure to the end, resist Satan's schemes, and succeed!

Some of us may lose our lives as a witness for Christ. So what? If we have allowed Christ to work true salvation into us, then there will be no sting (pain) in death. (Remember Stephen in Acts 6:8-7:60) God expects His church to endure through much of the Great Tribulation and testify as to Christ, His great love and His redemptive plan. When the last great harvest of souls is complete, as Satan's full fury comes against the world peaks during the Great Tribulation, then you can expect His appearance to quickly call us up, for we are not destined for wrath or to be condemned to judgment with the world.

"For the Lord himself will descend from heaven with a cry of command, with the archangel's call, and with the sound of the trumpet of God. And the dead in Christ will rise first; then we who are alive, who are left, shall be caught up together with them in the clouds to meet the Lord in the air; and so we shall always be with the Lord. Therefore comfort one another with these words. But as to the times and the seasons, brethren, you have no need to have anything written to you. For you yourselves know well that the day of the Lord will come like a thief in the night. When people say, 'There is peace and security,' then sudden destruction will come upon them as travail comes upon a woman with child, and there will be no escape. But you are not in darkness, brethren, for that day to surprise you like a thief. For you are all sons of light and sons of the day; we are not of the night or of darkness. So then let us not sleep, as others do, but let us keep awake and be sober. For those who sleep sleep at night, and those

who get drunk are drunk at night. But, since we belong to the day, let us be sober, and put on the breastplate of faith and love, and for a helmet the hope of salvation. For God has not destined us for wrath, but to obtain salvation through our Lord Jesus Christ, who died for us so that whether we wake or sleep we might live with him. Therefore encourage one another and build one another up, just as you are doing" (1 Thessalonians 4:16- 5:11).

The great day of Christ's wrath is coming. We are not destined for His wrath. The Great Tribulation is nothing compared to the wrath of God.

"When he opened the sixth seal, I looked, and behold, there was a great earthquake; and the sun became black as sackcloth, the full moon became like blood, and the stars of the sky fell to the earth as the fig tree sheds its winter fruit when shaken by a gale; the sky vanished like a scroll that is rolled up, and every mountain and island was removed from its place. Then the kings of the earth and the great men and the generals and the rich and the strong, and every one, slave and free, hid in the caves and among the rocks of the mountains, calling to the mountains and rocks, 'Fall on us and hide us from the face of him who is seated on the throne, and from the wrath of the Lamb; for the great day of their wrath has come, and who can stand before it?'" (Revelation 6:12-17).

Indeed, we hear the thunder of the horsemen of the Apocalypse. September 11 was a major milestone for the end-of-the-age sequencing ordained by God! *REVELATION SIX* horrors are approaching fast. Let us be sober and get ready so that we will not be ashamed at His coming and left behind to suffer God's wrath! AMEN and AMEN!

About the Author

Charles Pretlow has nearly two decades experience in ministry and pastoral counseling. He completed his basic Bible classes at Seattle Pacific College and finished his undergraduate work at Central Washington University.

It was in 1973, while in the Marines, that he came to know Christ. In the ensuing years, he has seen much trouble, abuse, and confusion within the body of Christ. He has years of experience and study in practical theology, working in a ministerial capacity with evangelical, Pentecostal and charismatic congregations, as well as independent fellowships. In 1988, he founded a non-denominational ministry, emphasizing pastoral counseling that incorporated sound biblical principles to help Christians cooperate with God in the sanctification and healing process that God gives through Jesus Christ.

Over these years of ministry, he has dealt with a wide spectrum of Christians who complained of a troubled walk with Christ. He dealt with many severe cases and developed a scriptural understanding concerning the source of their difficulties.

Since his conversion 1973, he has overcome his own obstacles and challenges that, like so many others, prevent Christians from coming to the full grace of God and a stable life in Christ. His ministry is practical—helping others work out their salvation, leaning on the Lord, and sharing from his own healing process and experiences.

The main thrust of ministry is to help the sincere Christian prepare for the coming trouble leading to Christ's appearance.

Workshops, seminars, and other ministry venues by the author are available to further equip pastors, leaders, and Christian workers for the coming final true move of God and the ensuing trouble leading to the rapture of those who are truly Christ's own.

Ministry Information

For workshop and ministry engagements information

Wilderness Voice Ministries - **www.wvministries.com**

Speaking and ministry schedules are subject to change.

Online Chapel Fellowship Service

At Message of the Cross Ministries International

Access online live fellowship and resources, at - **www.motci.com**

MORE BOOKS
BY *Charles Pretlow*

The Horsemen Cometh - Gloom, Doom, or Glory? This is a startling work that confronts the spell over God's people with biblical truth; the truth about the end of this age that should excite the sincere Christian. However, many are blinded and held captive by false teachings, for them the truth is terrifying and gloomy, thus it is avoided, denied and even attacked. This work will help equip the true saint for the coming trouble leading to Christ's appearance.

Wake Up Now - *Before the midnight cry!* Learn from the parables of the wise and foolish: the wise maidens were ready, but the foolish were not and were locked out of heaven. The wise man built his foundation for life upon the rock; the foolish man built upon sand and lost everything. Learn how to be ready and how to work out your own salvation and grow up into the fullness of Christ.

Call to be Lead by Example Many are called to lead, but few have opportunity to learn how to pastor and disciple others. This work is an excellent resource to help guide those called to minister the Gospel of Christ. Home cell leaders, independent home fellowship pastors, or small to medium size congregation leaders—this work is an effective leadership and mentoring resource.

Other Tract-Book Titles

America on the Brink – *A nation afflicted before the final judgment*
Effective Spiritual Warfare - *Learn to resist and fight the devil in the true power of Christ*
Last Days Sorcery - *The powers of darkness unleashed and magnified through the human spirit*
Remember Lot's Wife - *Give up the world and don't look back!*
Simon the Magician Christians - *Help for those in bondage to marketing the counterfeit power of God*
The Pre-Tribulation Rapture Lie - *Are you at risk of being LOCKED out!*

Tract-Book Bulk Discount Orders for Your Ministry

Wilderness Voice Publishing makes available bulk orders at discount for those led by the Lord to use these messages in their ministry.

Tract-Book titles are designed to help those Christian that confused concerning the truth of Christ's coming and to form a solid understanding of all the teaching of Christ.

Contact Midnight Voice Publishing to receive bulk order quantity discount pricing. - **www.wildernesspublishing.com**

www.ingramcontent.com/pod-product-compliance
Lightning Source LLC
Chambersburg PA
CBHW020025050426
42450CB00005B/643